More In_ Readings for the Christian Woman

Spiritual Warfare: Breaking the FAADS (Fear-Anger-Anxiety-Depression Syndrome)

Carolyn Baldwin Tucker, Ph.D.

ISBN: 978-0-89098-889-3

©2018 by 21st Century Christian
2809 12th Ave S, Nashville, TN 37204
All rights reserved.

Cover design by Jonathan Edelhuber

TABLE OF CONTENTS

FOREWORD

God wants us to be saved and to live eternally with Him in heaven. He wants this so strongly that He sent His only begotten Son to die for us so that one day we will be able to live with Him forever (John 3:16).

There is a war being waged by the devil against us so that he can ultimately win our souls to him. The primary function and goal of our chief adversary (the devil) is to destroy our faith, deceive our minds, and ultimately, steal our souls so that we would be tormented with him forever (John 10:10). The devil uses the seed of deception as one of his foremost tricks and when that seed is planted, he waters it with fear. Because fear is a restrictive, binding spirit, the devil plays on our fears to gain further control of our minds causing the FAADS (fear, anger, anxiety, depression) to develop.

Once fear is added to deception, we can see anger having the doorway for entry. When people realize they have been deceived, they become fearful of what will happen as a result of the deception. They become angry and upset because of the deception. If the anger is not expressed by the one who feels that emotion, that anger is turned inward, causing anxiety because of not having been able to express the anger outwardly or to deal with the anger in an effective manner. Anxiety begins to creep in causing worry and feelings of rejection; those are soon followed by doubt and stress. Shortly after anxiety has begun to manifest itself, the spirit of depression begins to settle in, leading the Christian to become insecure or unsure of herself and others. Unless there is an intervention, that person may become so depressed that she begins to question the reality of God or the need for her existence.

These tricks of the devil form the basis for spiritual warfare and are rooted in the seed of deception, that is cultivated by fear. Once satan has us fearful, angry, anxious and depressed, we begin to spiral deeper and deeper into the FAADS (Fear, Anger, Anxiety, Depression Syndrome).

Acknowledgements and Dedication

This book is written to glorify God, His Son—our Savior, Jesus Christ, and the Holy Spirit who provide strength, comfort, peace, and direction as we engage in spiritual warfare with our adversary, the devil.

To my husband, Jesse Tucker, who has always supported and encouraged me in my efforts, I express sincere love and appreciation. To our children, Susan Tucker Jones and Randall (Ericca) Tucker, I thank you for being my crowns of glory and personifying the fruit of our labor. To our four grandchildren (Josiah, Randall, Alani, and Rylan) who are truly blessings, I pray that God will always guide you; leading you in the "paths of righteousness."

Forever, I will be grateful for my parents, Mr. George and Mrs. Susie Baldwin, who provided the kind of examples of sustenance and courage which would serve our family long after their earthly presence ended. May God forever bless my sister, Jewell Baldwin Cousin, who reared me from preteen years until early adulthood. I pray favor for my other siblings who have continuously been sources of support and encouragement to me: James (Lorene) Baldwin; Evelyn Baldwin Johnson; John (Ruby) Baldwin; Irene Baldwin Chapman; Marion E. Baldwin; and Gilbert (Janice) Baldwin. To my many nieces and nephews, thank you for continuing the Baldwin legacy.

In memory of my husband's parents, Mr. Tom and Mrs. Josephine Tucker, I am thankful for the legacy they left for my husband and his siblings.

"To God Be the Glory."

SPIRITURAL WARFARE

For the Christian, this type warfare is fought
by use of Godly weapons.
We are waging war against the devil
for the salvation of our souls.
To be victorious, we must be armed with
the Word of God.

CHAPTER 1
SPIRITUAL WARFARE

The Christian must remember that God did not give us a "spirit of fear," but He gives us the spirit of "power, love and a sound mind" (2 Timothy 1:7). Therefore, as Christians, we should not be intimidated or fearful of what is threatened by the enemy. We should be bold in our faith, holding fast to the assurances that God has given us. When the spirits of fear, anger, anxiety, and depression come against us, we must be ready to wage defensive warfare against those wiles (tricks) of the devil. To engage in defensive warfare, we must be fully clothed in the armor of the Lord (Ephesians 6:10-18) and know how to use our weapons.

Knowing and applying Scripture to our lives allows us to be secure when dealing with the forces of evil. We must be able to effectively use our sword (the Word of God). The best defense against a lie (the devil's chief deceptive ploy) is the truth. Truth is the first part of the spiritual armor cited in the passage listed in Ephesians 6:14, "the girdle of truth." If you are supported, encased, and fortified by "truth," the lies of the deceiver will not hurt you, nor will those lies survive. Truth will stand when all else fails. Truth is not dependent upon any other force because it exists in and of itself; being fully manifested although all of the forces of evil attack it. Truth will stand because when we profess truth, we profess Christ. Jesus said, "I am the way the

2

TRUTH and the life...." (John 14:6). Truth is the weapon that sets us free: free from the bondages of the devil, free from the impact of his lies, and free to be whole in Christ (John 8:32).

Any spirit that is not of God is of the devil. The spirits of fear, anger, anxiety, and depression are the fruit of the devil. The fruit of God is found in love, joy, peace,... (Galatians 5:22-23). Those are the fruit that we must seek to have as part of our daily lives. Fear, anger, anxiety, and depression are toxic spirits born in the spirit of satan. In satan we find no healing balm for those in need of a solace. Those toxic spirits are poison to our spirit being and will destroy the minds of those who feast on their fumes.

The name of Jesus is powerful and is a defense against the negative spirits of satan. The name of Jesus commands all authority. "That at the name of Jesus every knee will bow...and every tongue will confess that Jesus Christ is Lord..."(Philippians 2:10-12). Hearing the Word and believing that Jesus is the Christ brings us to a place where we are on the threshold of becoming a Christian. Repentance of sin, confession of faith in Jesus, and baptism with Him position us to receive the blessings of the faithful and protection against the one who goes about "seeking whom he may devour" (1 Peter 5:8). There is nothing that can stand in opposition to the mighty name of Jesus. Neither the devil nor his demons can withstand the name of Jesus. When demons hear the name of Jesus, they tremble (James 2:19).

Christians who want to overcome the negative strongholds of satan must think on good things. Thinking on good things blocks negative thoughts from bombarding the mind (Philippians 4:8). As Christian women, we must clothe our minds with the Word of God and pray His promises, knowing that we have already received deliverance. We must ask the dear Lord to order our steps in His Word and not let evil have rule over us (Psalm 119:133).

The Word of God is our strong defense in the battle for our minds. There is no way satan can successfully wage war against us if we are fully armed with the Word of God. There are numerous Scriptures available to us, which serve as solid ground for our defense (1 Corinthians 10:13; Romans 12:2; 1 John 4:1; 1 Corinthians 6:19-20; 1 John 1:9; James 5:16).

Empowered by her relationship with Christ, the Christian woman will stand boldly against the wiles of the devil; holding fast to the thought, *I know that I am a victor and not a victim because "in all things, I am more than a conqueror"!* (Romans 8:37). Fear will not hold her hostage nor will it overtake the good that God has planned for her to do (Jeremiah 29:10). She will not be doubtful, nor will she allow fearful thoughts to dominate her mind. By standing boldly on her convictions, she will not be subjected to the tricks of the devil nor his spirits of fear, anger, anxiety, and depression (Ephesians 6:13).

Read and speak the following Scriptures on a daily basis so that you, your family, and other loved ones can hear the power of the Word: "Faith cometh by hearing and hearing by the word of God" (Romans 10:17). It is important that the Word is spoken because there is power in the Word of God. God spoke this world into existence and through knowledge and use of His Word, we are able to speak to circumstances in our lives praying the promises found in the Word of God, and we will see the changes that will occur as a result. When we pray the promises of God, we are praying the will of God (1 Thessalonians 5:18). Whatever we ask according to His will, He will grant: "And this is the confidence that we have in him, that if we ask any thing according to his will, he hearth us" (1 John 5:14-15).

Declarations of Faith Based on the Sword of the Spirit

1. I will be careful of the words that I speak. Proverbs 6:2 says, "Thou art snared by the words of thy mouth."

2. I will study God's Word and let it be a part of our daily life, knowing that God's Word is true and His promises are always fulfilled. Isaiah 55:10-11 says, "For as the rain cometh down, and the snow from heaven, and returneth not thither, but watereth the earth, and maketh it bring forth and bud, that it may give seed to the sower, and bread to the eater: So shall my word be that goeth forth out of my mouth; it shall not return unto me void, but it shall accomplish that which I please, and it shall prosper in the things whereunto I sent it."

3. God will provide for my needs in the manner and time He so desires. Philippians 4:19 says, "But my God shall supply all your need according to his riches in glory by Christ Jesus."

4. I will not allow fear nor doubt be proclaimed over me. I will not allow the negative predictions of others keep me from praying and asking God to provide for my needs. Jeremiah 29:12-13 says, "Then shall ye call upon me and ye shall go and pray unto me, and I will hearken unto you."

5. I will rely on the Holy Spirit to empower me to do the things that are good and that God wants me to do. Romans 8:26 says, "Likewise, the Spirit also helpeth our infirmities for we know not what we should pray for as we ought, but the Spirit itself maketh intercession for us with groanings which cannot be uttered."

6. As a Christian, I am to walk in the anointing of Christ. First John 2:27 says, "But the anointing which ye have received of him abideth in you, and ye need not that any man teach you, but as the same anointing teacheth you of all things and is truth, and no lie, and even as it hath taught you, ye shall abide in him."

7. I will not allow anyone to make me feel as if I cannot be successful in the good things that I want to do because Philippians 4:13 says, "I can do all things through Christ which strengtheneth me."

8. I will give to others freely; I will give to those in need and will not expect that they should repay me. Luke 6:38 teaches, "Give, and it shall be given unto you; good measure pressed down, and shaken together, and running over, shall men give unto your bosom. For with the same measure that ye mete withal it shall be measured to you again."

9. Jesus does not want me to be sick. Matthew 4:23 says, "And Jesus went about all Galilee, teaching in their synagogues, and preaching the gospel of the kingdom, and healing all manner of sickness and all manner of disease among the people."

10. When I pray, I know that God will hear and answer my prayer. Isaiah 65:24 says, "And it shall come to pass

that before they call, I will answer, and while they are yet speaking, I will hear."

11. I will not be defeated by the circumstances that are before me. I will continue to pray and believe in God because Roman 8:37 says, "Nay, in all these things we are more than conquerors through him that loved us."

12. I will not worry over situations or circumstances that exist in my life. I will rely on Philippians 4:6-7, which says, "Be careful for nothing; but in everything by prayer and supplication with thanksgiving let your requests be made known unto God. And the peace of God which passeth all understanding shall keep your hearts and minds through Christ Jesus."

13. I will not live in fear and doubt because it is said in 2 Timothy 1:7, "God did not give us a spirit of fear but of power, and of love and a sound mind."

14. I will not put my faith in others to be always truthful with me because I know what is said in Proverbs 3:5-6: "Trust in the Lord with all thine heart and lean not to thine own understanding, in all thy ways acknowledge him and he will direct thy path."

15. When people mistreat me, I will not seek to "pay them back" because Psalm 37:1-2 says, "Fret not thyself over evil doers and be thou not envious of workers of iniquity, for they soon shall be cut down like the grass and wither as the green herb."

16. I will not walk in the way of the world but daily focus on how I can renew my mind through a focus on the word of God (Romans 12:2).

17. I will read my Bible daily and not listen to what the people of this world have to say about trying to live a Christian life. I will not allow them to lead me astray because Psalm 1:1-2 says, "Blessed is the man that walketh not in the counsel of the ungodly, nor standeth in the way of sinners, nor sitteth in the seat of the scornful, but his delight is in the law of the Lord and in his law doth the meditate day and night."

18. I will be thankful and give praises to the Lord for whatever circumstance in which I find myself. Psalm 34:1-2 says, "I will bless the Lord at all times, his praise shall continually be in my mouth."

19. I will not fear for my safety but wholly trust in the Lord because Psalm 4:8 says, "I will both lay me down in peace and sleep for the Lord, only makest me dwell in safety."

20. I will pray to the Lord for the safety of me and my family. I will not worry about the safety because Psalm 91:5-7 says, "Thou shalt not be afraid of the terror by night nor for the arrow that flieth by day. Nor for the pestilence that walketh in darkness, nor for the destruction that wasteth at noonday. A thousand shall fall at thy side, and ten thousand at thy right hand, but it shall not come nigh to thee."

21. I will praise the Lord when things are going well and when they are not going well because I know the Scripture, Romans 8:28, that says, "And we know that all things work together for good to them that love God and to them who are the called according to his purpose."

22. I will not allow sickness to overtake me because I know that Isaiah 53:5 says, "But he was wounded for our transgressions, he was bruised for our iniquities, the chastisement of our peace was upon him, and with his stripes we are healed."

23. I know that good things await me if I remain faithful during my times of trial because Psalm 84:11 says, "For the Lord God is a sun and shield; the Lord will give grace and glory; no good thing will he withhold from them that walk uprightly."

24. I will not be envious of those who prosper nor be depressed when I am not progressing in health or wealth as I think I should because I remember Job 14:14 says, "...all the days of my appointed time will I wait till my change come."

25. I will not be disappointed if I don't get that promotion for which I have applied: It just may not be my time because I know that Psalm 75:6 says, "For promotion cometh neither from the east, nor from the west, nor from the south. But God is the judge; he putteth down one and setteth up another."

Discussion Questions:

1. Why do so many Christians fall victim to the tricks of the devil?

2. What weapons does the Christian have as a defense in this spiritual warfare?

3. Why is it that the devil is able to deceive so many people?

4. What are some affirmations that the Christian woman can make and be assured they are true?

5. How does the devil use lies to cause fear, unrest, and turmoil?

6. How can older Christians provide support for younger Christians?

7. Identify seven Scriptures cited in this chapter that can help reassure a fellow Christian that by God's grace we are able to overcome evil that may be done to us.

PERSONAL SPIRITUAL ARMOR

The personal spiritual armor that is worn by the Christrian must be a part of the internal fabric of the Christian. Through following God's Word and letting it guide us in all that we do, we are equipping ourselves with the armor of the Lord, which is vital to our spiritual survival.

(Ephesians 6:10-16)

CHAPTER 2
PERSONAL ARMOR: FORTIFIED BY THE WORD

As a Christian, I know that I am dependent on the Word of God for my strength, direction, discernment, and clarity of mind. As a Christian woman who has been truly blessed by the Lord to have been successful in life's endeavors, I can attest to the fact that daily I utilize the spiritual armor of the Lord and without it, I would not be able to thrive in this world that has been subdued by the deceptions of the devil (Revelations 12:9).

The Word of God is powerful, and when I read it, believe it, obey it, and practice it, I am empowered. The Word of God allows me to have peace and helps me to drive out evil, oppressive spirits (fear, anger, anxiety, depression) that want to take up residence in my mind (Isaiah 26:3). When David was in anguish about the destruction of Ziglag and his men wanted to stone him, he encouraged himself in the Lord (1 Samuel 30:6). Sometimes we must encourage ourselves, and there is no greater way to be encouraged than by the reading of the Word and by remembering how God has brought us through difficulties in the past. I use the Word of God as both my defense and my offense against the wiles (the tricks) of the devil. By use of the Word of God and my faith in God, I have been able to withstand the "fiery darts" the evil one constantly hurls at me, but which have found no resting place in my spirit.

There have been situations in which people have tried to use deception to cause me to believe a lie. But by the grace of God and the Spirit of God, I have been able to discern the truth and see the deception they try to hide (Romans 8:26-27). I have come to know, that if there is any portion of a story that I have found to be untrue, I cannot believe the story. I must be careful to not be deceived by partial truths but to "dig a little deeper" into the essence of the situation.

The Lord also blessed me to have a life assignment as an educator. As an educator and former principal, I have experienced many situations involving parents and children. I learned early in my profession to listen closely to the recounting of events that children give and how they did or did not commit an offense. After forty-eight years of being an educator, I have learned there is an element of truth in each story that is told, and my task is to determine what that element is and how it plays into the larger scheme of events as related to truth. During my years as a principal, I relied heavily on the discernment of the Holy Spirit. By reading my Bible daily and praying for wisdom constantly (James 1:5), I was successful in my roles as teacher, principal, supervisor and a director of elementary schools. By the grace of God, I know the practical side and reality of a reliance on the Holy Spirit for guidance (Jeremiah 10:23).

I have found that parents are often confused about what is best for their children. In trying to communicate their concern for the well-being of their children, they may become emotional and appear angry. I have learned that a little patience, a calm voice, careful selection of my words, and a willingness to listen to their story can change a potentially volatile situation into one of meaning and understanding (Proverbs 15:1).

By the grace of God, I have been able to be victorious even when it seemed the odds were against me. When realizing the weakness and frailty of my own strength, I remember the words to Paul and my weakness allows Christ to become my strength (2 Corinthians 12:9).

There is power in speaking the Word. When my words line up with God's Word, I find situations seem less complex, storms are a little weaker, and peace is ushered into my midst. Words that are used in given situations can either escalate an adverse situation or bring calm to those involved in a situation.

When I am troubled regarding situations, I try not to worry but remember the advice given by Paul to the Philippians regarding not worrying about anything but in essence "praying about everything" (Philippians 4: 6-7). Also, I remember the Scripture that tells me to give thanks in every situation and to pray without ceasing (1 Thessalonians 5:17-18). By being thankful, even in trying or difficult situations, I allow my faith to be made manifest. I must believe, even though I cannot see the end result, that the end will be positive for me because I know the positive works with the negative and results in what is good for me (Romans 8:28).

From the account given of the disciples and Jesus at sea as a storm was raging, I know that one command from the Master causes all things to get in order: "Peace, be still." The sea calmed its waves, and the winds ceased their blowing. In that statement Jesus called forth "Peace," and when He called forth "Peace," everything else had to "be still" (Mark 4:39). Jesus can cause that same peace to come into our lives and replace turbulence with calm. Jesus can

14

speak peace into our lives and into the chaos that seems to want to overtake our homes. Jesus' words are powerful and commanding. When we speak the words of Jesus and we rely on the power of His name, we are able to see circumstances change and situations improve (John 14:27).

God has sustained me in so many endeavors and has allowed me to experience wonderful blessings. As a Christian woman who was elected to public office and served eight years in that office, I often found the need to pray for inner strength, resolve, and direction. Against great odds and limited funds, by the grace of God and with the support of my husband, family, and friends, I mounted two successful campaigns for a countywide office. I know it was God taking the little funds that I had and multiplying them so that I had sufficiency to run the race. I had opportunity to see firsthand how God can take little and bless it so that it becomes plenty (Luke 9:12-17).

As an elected official I had to make decisions that would impact the lives of citizens who elected me and those who did not. I knew my votes had to be cast using the most accurate information available on any given subject, and answer the question, "How will this impact children and families?" My love for children and my love for families, predicated on my love for God, formed the basis upon which I cast my votes.

Many times, I received harsh criticism by fellow elected officials and the media for not "going along just to get along" and for taking the positions that would benefit children and families rather than the "wheelers and dealers." Many times, I was the lone *no* vote, but that did not bother me because I was fortified with the conviction of doing what I knew to do that was right, while praying for the Lord's protection and guidance. I knew that God would fight my battles (2 Chronicles 20:15) and uphold me with the right hand of His righteousness (Isaiah 41:10). Since having served in an elected position as a public official, I better understand the Scriptures that encourage Christians to pray for those who are our leaders (1 Timothy 2:1-2). Without the prayers of the saints, my time as an elected official would have been a lot more wearisome.

In my walk with the Lord, I have come to know that I must fill my mind with His words and His assurances as I am on this Christian journey. As a daily practice, I rely on God and the authority that I find in the name of Jesus, which allows me to stand against the deceptions, tricks, and evil plots of the devil. Over the years, I have developed affirmations that are supported by Scripture, and I use these in my daily walk. These Scriptures are powerful, and in them, I find encouragement for resisting the forces of evil and minimizing the affect that those wiles have on me as one who is trying to live a Christian life.

I know there is power in Jesus' name. Unclean spirits, demonic forces, and the host of satan's army are no match for the name of Jesus. In Jesus' name, by His authority, by the shedding of His blood and the confessing of sins, people are released from bondages and unhealthy thought patterns are ended; thus, the healing of the mind is begun. Deliverance from strongholds and ungodly soul ties can be accomplished by the surrendering of ourselves to the power of Jesus (2 Corinthians 10:3-5). Below are some declarations of faith in the mighty name of Jesus, which have become a part of my daily Christian walk:

1. In the name of Jesus, I command the spirits of fear, anger, anxiety and depression to leave. I speak to those toxic spirits of doubt and worry, commanding them to leave. "You have no authority to be here." When faced with challenges, I will not fear because fear can keep me from moving forward. It will restrict my thought process and render me less effective in my Christian walk. Fear will not find a resting place in my spirit. No unhealthy thoughts will invade the portals of my mind (**2 Timothy 1:7**).

2. In the name of Jesus, I command all of my thoughts to line up with the Word of God. I will think on good things. I will not allow gossip and rumors to dominate my thinking, and I will not be a part of spreading rumors because they will not overtake my thought process. When my thoughts line up with the Word of God, I can be at peace even in the middle of a storm. Aligning my thoughts with the Word of God is essential for me to remain focused in the presence of uncertainties. Alignment of my thoughts with the Word of God will prove beneficial as I continue in faith while in the midst of adverse situations. My thoughts will control my actions and behavior (**Philippians 4:8**).

3. In the name of Jesus, I confess all sins and wrongdoing that I have committed, which have caused negative situations in my life. The confessing of sin relieves me from the bondage of sin. It allows me to be free from guilt and depression over a sin that I committed. True repentance, the turning away from my sins, allows me to break the sin-hold and be under the blessed hold of Jesus (**James 5:16**).

4. In the name of Jesus, I declare peace and calm in my life. The peace that can be mine through Jesus far outweighs any pleasure that may be received from a life of sin. Christ can speak peace into my life. Peace takes reign over a troublesome atmosphere. Peace rides precedent over winds of hate, billows of negativism, and torments of pain. When I pray to God through Jesus, I ask Him to move in my life, to quiet the storms that are raging within me; when He speaks peace to the situations, I need to be still and listen. Anything that is contrary to peace must cease. Nothing can rise up against the peace that Jesus speaks into my life. Christ speaks this peace through His Word. Jesus told us "my peace of give you" (**John 14:27**), which should cause us to rejoice even in the midst of uncertainty because we know that Jesus' peace can calm any situation. Peace will prevail, and there is no force that satan has which can overtake the peace of Jesus. If we keep our minds focused on Jesus, we will be in perfect peace (**Isaiah 26:3**).

5. In the name of Jesus, I refuse to listen to unwise advice. There are many instances when people want to give advice that I have not requested nor believe is beneficial to my well being. I will not rely on their unwise advice, but I will seek the direction of the Lord. I will read His Word daily and meditate upon those precepts, knowing that direction and guidance can be found in the pages of inspiration. I know that if I rely and meditate on His Word, I will have a sense of calm and assurance even though in the natural, it seems as if the situation may be getting worse. My reliance and faith will come through pages of inspiration (**Psalm 1:1-6**).

6. In the name of Jesus, I will block and bind all negative thoughts, placing them at the feet of Jesus. When I am thinking about positive things that will enhance my walk with Christ, I will not allow those negative, toxic thoughts to hijack my joy nor invade the threshold of my mind. I will block those thoughts with the Word of God and quickly bring them into the obedience of Christ. Negative thoughts will not linger and take root in my mind. They will be uprooted by the Word of God and the power of His might (**2 Corinthians 10:5**).

7. In the name of Jesus, I confess that He is Lord above all and that His power and might strengthen me against the evil one. When Jesus rose, He rose with all power, and He has not relinquished any of it to satan. Therefore, satan has no power over me because my Lord and Savior Jesus Christ reigns supreme in my life. Through Him, I can overcome any obstacle (**Philippians 4:13**).

When I read the Scriptures, speak positive words, and think on good things, the devil will not find a boarding place in my mind. By doing those acts, I am fortifying my mind with the Word of God and where God's Word abides, there is no place for satan. Reliance on the Word of God allows me to be fully clothed in spiritual armor and to be fully equipped for the battle.

I have found that as I dress for the work-a-day world, I must also have myself spiritually clothed with God's armor so that I can make it through the trials of the day. I must wear the belt of truth to counter deception and the garment of righteousness to remain focused on and in right standing with what God wants me to do. I must walk in peace, refusing to be drawn into arguments and disputes. My shield of faith must be oiled with the spirit of joy and ready to be used against the attacks of the enemy. My head must be covered with the knowledge that I am saved by Jesus' blood and that I am striving to make heaven my home. By no means will I leave the house without my weapon of choice—the Bible. I most assuredly will have that continuous important conversation (prayer) with God, as I step out the door to face the world, the devil, and his dedicated workers (Ephesians 6:10-18).

In an effort to prepare for the tricks and plots of the devil, as a Christian I have to be ready to do spiritual battle and be equipped with the weapons of spiritual power. The devil seeks every opportunity he can find to try to confuse those who want to follow Christ. When all else fails, the devil will crank up the "fear mill" to cause the Christian to doubt or second guess things that are clear and right. Below is the mantra I developed as an offense to the mind games that the devil likes to play.

My Mantra

I will walk in the anointing of the Lord, undaunted by threats of the adversary. I have no fear of him because the one that I serve is Jehovah El Shaddai (God Almighty).

Though the forces of evil come against me, I will stand guarded by the whole armor of God. My speech will be that of truth; my life will reflect the spirit of supplication; and I will trod in the path of light, which is provided by my Lord and Savior Jesus Christ.

Empowered by the Holy Spirit, I will move through the torrents of criticism without fear because I hold forward the shining shield of faith. Salvation will be my helmet and will cause all of the attacks against me to be futile. I will cut away all strongholds and evil forces with the sword of the Spirit, boldly facing and triumphantly overcoming all the deceitful plots against me because God did not give me a spirit of fear but of "power, love and of a sound mind."

Nothing will come of those judgmental, toxic, counterfeit schemes that are intended against me by those who conspire to put evil in my path. Naught will come of their wicked imaginations because I am protected by the Angel of the Lord who encamps around me. The ministering spirits of God will protect me from the wiles of the devil.

I will walk in His Anointing, led by the Holy Spirit, upheld by His righteous right hand, cradled in His love, protected by His Word, healed by His stripes, and covered in the blood of the Lamb.

In Jesus' name will I joyously proclaim His Word to those who will receive Him. With prayer, supplication, and thanksgiving will I praise the One who controls all things and renders righteous judgment. Blessed be the name of the Lord Jesus Christ who will save me in the end. I give all praise, glory, and honor to God "from whom all blessings flow" for "He is worthy to be praised" forever and ever.

It is in the mighty name of JESUS that I render this declaration:

Amen and Amen!

Discussion Questions:

1. Why does the devil want to invade the minds of Christians?

2. What is a strong defense to the attacks of the devil?

3. Identify three things that you can do to improve your Christian service.

4. How can fellow sisters assist one another on their Christian journey?

5. How does spiritual armor differ from armor that is worn by our military?

6. After reading the chapter on personal armor, do you find any places in your spiritual armor that need reinforcing?

7. Identify seven Scriptures from this chapter that can strengthen you in your personal walk.

OVERCOMING FEAR WITH FAITH

Fear is a spirit that restricts the productive, positive actions of a Believer. However, faith conquers fear and arrests all its powers.

CHAPTER 3
OVERCOMING FEAR WITH FAITH

When we read Scripture, we can find many accounts of how the people of God trusted His Word and succeeded in their efforts through faith; even though those efforts seemed impossible, everything is possible with God. Belief that God is able to do what He said He would do allows the Christian to move forward when all indicators say there is no way to accomplish the task. The one who does this is operating out of faith and has placed fear on hold. Faith allows the believer to do things that otherwise she would not do (Esther 4:16).

God had allowed Daniel and his three Hebrew friends—Shadrach, Meshach, and Abednego—who were in captivity in Babylon to find favor in the sight of the king, placing them over provinces in the Babylonian kingdom (Daniel 2). Continuing in the book of Daniel, we find those three Hebrew children were thrown into the fiery furnace because they would not bow down to the graven image that the king had made even though they knew what fate awaited them. They told the king that their God was able to save them from the furnace but even if He did not, still they would not bow down before the golden image. God delivered the three Hebrew boys from the fiery furnace because of their faith. He did not allow them to burn or to have the smell of smoke to be on them after then came out of the furnace (Daniel 3).

24

We also read about Daniel and how God delivered him. Of course, when Daniel was placed in the lion's den, it was a surety that Daniel would be eaten by the lions. But belief and reliance on God in the exercise of faith allowed Daniel to be saved from the lions as God dispatched an angel to shut the mouths of the lions. (Daniel 5:8-22). If Daniel had any fear (and there is no indication that he did), it was overshadowed by his unyielding faith and allegiance to God. Daniel knew that the God he served was able to do all things; therefore, he had no need to fear. Though Daniel was faced with the threat of certain death, his faith did not waver, and fear had no hold on him. Daniel prayed and found peace in his trial. He did not worry about the lions, because he was protected by the angel of the Lord (Psalm 34:7). "Daniel was not in the lions' den; the lions were in Daniel's den" because he was able to sleep peacefully, and the lions had no power over Daniel (Daniel 6).

Today, thank God, we do not have to face the actual fiery furnace or the den of lions, but we do have trials and situations that cause us to have to draw on our faith. Sometimes the "fiery furnace" of criticism and ridicule by others can cause us to fear the circumstances of life. Our faith may be challenged by co-workers or by bosses who want us to participate in activities that are not becoming to Christians. May times ultimatums are given that "if you don't do this, or "if you don't do that, you will be fired." If those demands violate the principles of Christianity, that is the time for us to stand our ground and to be faithful, not fearful (Hebrews 6:10-11).

Each day we hear news reports of foreclosures, unem-ployment, and families in distress. For those with no hope, with no faith, such news can be devastating. However, the

Christian woman, though living *in* this world, is not *of* this world and is not controlled by the fear attached to those negative news reports (2 Corinthians 10:3). She knows that there is good news (the gospel), which is able to calm fears, raise hopes, and secure fainting hearts.

The knowledge that faith has power over fear is comforting to the Christian. Faith in the fact that God always fulfills His promises and provides for those who are His (Philippians 4:19) is reassuring to the Christian. Faith allows the Christian not to be controlled by the circumstances that are seen, but by the God who is unseen.

If the Christian woman wants her faith to overtake her fears, she must feed her faith and starve her fears. She feeds her faith by reading a healthy, daily portion of the Word of God (Psalm 1:1-2). She allows her soul to feast on the good things of the Bible. In doing so, she does not allow opportunities for fear to grow: for where fear is not nourished, it will not be able to thrive nor survive.

The fear of God is the only fear that is sanctioned by God. We are to fear Him and keep His commandments (Ecclesiastes 12:13). We are told that the beginning of our knowledge is the fear of the Lord (Proverbs 1:7). Therefore, if we fear anything or anyone else, we are taking what is reserved for God and allowing it to be used in a non-authorized manner. What belongs to God is reserved for Him and Him alone. Fear is reverence for God, and no one or no thing equates to the level of God (Proverbs 8:13; Psalm 33:8; Matthew 10:38; Luke 1:50; 1 Peter 2:17).

The devil wants to steal our faith. Fear and doubt are his main tools to cause us to become weak in the faith. Belief in Christ and the salvation that He offers are to be rooted in the faith that we have regarding God. The creation, the redemption of sinners by the blood of the lamb, and our hope of eternal life are all supporting factors for the faith that should lie within us. If the Christian woman allows her faith to be shaken to the point that she questions the existence of God, the devil will have gained another soul.

Negative thoughts and thoughts that are contrary to what God would have us think challenge our knowledge of Him. Fear of things or people is not real and goes against the teaching of God. When gone unchecked, fear can become a stronghold for a person and must be brought down and rendered powerless (2 Corinthians 10:3-5). If we hold fast to faith in God and His promises, we demonstrate to satan and all of his little demons that though satan is mighty, we know God is *Almighty*, and Jesus has overcome the world (1 John 5:4).

Throughout Scripture, we are told to "fear not," and "do not be afraid." When reviewing life situations, we should come to a clear conclusion: God does not want us to fear problems or circumstances that may be before us or obstacles that may be placed in our way. God does not want us to be fearful because fear is a restricting, binding spirit that will not allow the Christian to act out of faith. For reassurance and building of faith, we need to read the Scriptures, which are replete with verses to reassure us that God will strengthen us; He will help and uphold us (Isaiah 41:10).

When we read the Bible, we can find inspiration through the Scriptures as we see faith demonstrated by those who were obedient to God, even in the face of threats and death. King Hezekiah was challenged by the Assyrian king, Sennacherib, and sought word from the Lord because of the threats that had been made against him and the unholy words that he spoke against God. The prophet Isaiah sent word to Hezekiah not to fear because the Lord had heard his cry, and the Assyrian King would not be allowed to enter Jerusalem. God assured Hezekiah by saying through the prophet Isaiah that he would "put a hook in his nose and a bit in his lips and turn him back the way he came" (2 Kings 19:28-29). Sennacherib was sent in another direction because God had caused him to hear a rumor. Following that rumor, he lost his life. Hezekiah trusted God, had faith in His word, and did not allow the fear of man to overtake him. The God who protected Hezekiah is the same God who protects us (Hebrews 13:8). We must obey Him and allow our faith in Him to crush our fears of the world.

I know that when I have a difficult situation with which I am dealing, if I get stuck on how big the problem is, I cannot focus on how big God is. The devil is happy when he can get us off center, which means by losing focus on God and what He can do. Scripture teems with encouraging verses that tell us not to fear, but to rely on the power of the Lord: Isaiah 44:10; 2 Kings 6:16; Psalm 118:6; Proverbs 29:25; Romans 8:15; Hebrews 13:6; Luke 12:4-5.

Reflecting on my life and how God has brought me through many difficult situations (the death of my father when I was five and my mother dying on my 11th birthday) allows me to put current problems in prospective and know that when doing right, God will guide me past the obstacles and through the maze of distractions (Proverbs 3:5-6).

In difficult situations as we live in today's world, we find that people will disappoint us and fail to deliver on commitments they have promised. Often, we wonder if we should continue in an effort when it looks like all signs point to abandoning the idea. That is the time when the Christian should dig in with determination because the battle is almost won. Satan knows that, so he turns up the heat on problems, causing fear and doubt. But the Christian woman should pull on her faith and knowledge of God and how He has brought many followers through adverse situations. This may be the time for her to give thanks to God for trusting her to deal with this particular situation (1 Thessalonians 5:18). This is not the time for fear, but for faith.

Knowledge of the Old Testament and how God brought His people through the struggles of their day gives us a healthy appreciation for the way God can deliver us from evil forces that may want to come against us. We should have no fear but through faith wholly trust in God (Isaiah 41:10).

Just as He fought Joshua's battles, defeated Jehoshaphat's enemies, and caused Gideon to be triumphant over the Midianites because of their obedience, God is still faithful to His promises today if we are obedient to this word. Joshua believed that God was able to defeat the enemies of Israel. God was having Joshua to trust in Him for the victory. Jehoshaphat feared first, then called a fast and prayed to God for deliverance. Gideon was led by God to victory; although he was outnumbered by man, he was empowered by God. (Joshua 1: 5-8; 2 Chronicles 20:15-18; Judges 7:7).

When fear wants to set in regarding actions that I know I need to take even in the face of adversity, my strength is renewed when I reflect on women of the Bible such as Deborah. She went into battle to support the captain of Israel's army because he was afraid to go without her (Judges 4). Abigail had no fear when she rode off to meet David and kept him from avenging himself (1 Samuel 25:23-32).

Under the New Covenant today of grace and truth, Christians have two main advantages that the leaders of the Old Testament did not have under the old covenant. Those advantages are in the work that Jesus did on the cross, and the Holy Spirit who constantly makes intercession for us before the Father (Romans 8:3,4,26).

In overcoming fear, I have found that prayer is a powerful weapon. Praying to God, believing that my request will be granted (Matthew 21:2), relieves my fear and doubt. I believe prayer demonstrates to God that I know I cannot handle a situation without Him and that I know He is able. By praying and believing, I do not have time to fear. I remember the promise that Jesus gave His disciples when He told them they could ask whatever they wanted and it would be granted if they abided in Him and His words abided in them (John 15:7). Fear, which is a controlling spirit, does not have permission to be in my life. The only controlling spirit that I want or need in my life is the HOLY SPIRIT!

I try every day to fulfill the command of letting the Word of God dwell in me richly, and as a result, I trust the Lord to guide my steps, and I know He will not allow me to fear my situations (Colossians 3:16).

God knows our hearts, but we must speak the words of our confession so that others will know that we are His and that He is the center of our lives. Through speaking of God's protection and love for us, we let others know that it is not by our own strength that we do the things we do, but it is by the power of God who strengthens us and causes us not to fear. God will protect us and keep us from the pursuits of wicked people (Psalm 91).

For years, because of being concerned that people would think me strange, I did not share my conviction of faith with others and held it just to be a private matter. In doing so, I neglected the part of the Great Commission, which I could fulfill by sharing the good news with those with whom I had contact. Though I will never be an overseas missionary, nor lead a gospel crusade, I can still share the gospel of Jesus Christ with those in my small circle of associates. When asked how I have been able to be successful and where I find the energy to complete the tasks that I undertake, I now share Christ by letting the person know that it is by the grace of God that I do what I do. In doing so, I have an opportunity to share " the hope that lies" within me (1 Peter 3:15).

Not overcoming the fear of sharing our faith will hinder us from helping another soul escape the clutches of satan. This kind of fear is straight from the devil. He does not want us to tell others about Christ because in doing so, satan loses another battle in the war for man's soul. There is Scripture that tells us that saints will be saved by the blood that Jesus shed and the giving of their testimony (Revelation 12:11).

As heirs of the promise, we should not have fear of anything because Christ has conquered all things (Psalm 68:18). He overcame those things that would overcome us (Ephesians 4:8). We, as Christians, should have no fear because of our relationship with Christ. Through Christ we are heirs to the promise. God has fulfilled His promise through Jesus, our Savior and mediator (Galatians 3:16-29). This promise of blessing is now imparted to Christians today, and by faith we are partakers of the promise (Hebrews 6:13-14).

If we build our faith through a reliance and knowledge of the Word, our faith will topple our fears. As Christian women, we should strive to be faith builders and fear blockers.

FOCUSED FAITH ~ A Self-Examination

Discussion Questions:

1. Is faith working in my life?
2. Do I meditate on the Scriptures in an effort to increase my faith?
3. If confessing Christ meant that I would lose my job, would I acknowledge my relationship with Christ?
4. If my employer said that "practicing" Christians could not work there, would I still demonstrate Christianity?
5. Is Christianity so prevalent in my life that someone could look at my example, observe my lifestyle, listen to my speech, see how I dress, and conclude that I am a Christian?
6. If I were on trial today for being a Christian, would there be enough evidence to convict me?

7. What can I do to increase my faith?

INCREASING MY FAITH

To build my faith and focus my walk with Christ, I commit to doing this three-point plan:

1.

2.

3.

"The Best Examination Is a Self-Examination."

Discussion Questions:

1. Have you ever had to deal with your fears in a public manner?
2. What gives you comfort when facing your fears?
3. How can you help others deal with fear?
4. Why does God not want us to be fearful of circumstances or situations?
5. As you read accounts of great people of the Bible, who stands out most to you and why?
6. What fear do you see as the greatest hindrance to the spreading of God's Word?
7. List seven Scriptures presented in the chapter that will help you in dealing with fears.

CONTROLLING ANGER THROUGH PRAYER

Prayer is always in order; especially so when we find ourselves in a state of anger. Talking with God about the problems that cause us to be angry serves as a means of diffusing the anger. "Prayer is like oxygen to the soul" as it revives us and causes us to begin to get in right standing with God.

CHAPTER FOUR
CONTROLLING ANGER THROUGH PRAYER

Anger has its birth in dissatisfaction and/or disappointment. Often people become angry when their expectations have not been met when they have believed and trusted that those expectations would be realized. Some people have been disappointed so many times that a scowl or a frown is how they have come to interact with others. In such instances, their demeanor is that of hostility, impatience, and/or antagonism.

Have you ever been around someone who appears to always be angry? Have you ever tried to talk with someone who was angry? Do you feel uncomfortable when you are around someone who is angry? More than likely, you can answer *yes* to all those questions. Anger is a spirit that overtakes us when we do not allow the spirit of peace to prevail in our lives. Unresolved conflicts, unforgiveness, and holding on to hurt will have a negative impact upon the one who holds those feelings, as well as those around her (Ecclesiastes 7:9). This can be the source of internal conflict for that person. Anger is not of God but is of the devil who uses it to further his causes and purposes.

Anger may result from needs that have gone unmet and frustrations that have been allowed to mount. Feelings of rejection, ridicule, and embarrassment can be catalysts to anger. Determining the source and cause of the anger will assist the person in reducing situations that might lead to anger.

Although we have permission to be angry, we do not have permission to sin while we are angry (Ephesians 4:26). Christian women have an unending source for resolving anger: Jesus. He does not want us to be anger, hostile, or bitter. Clothing ourselves in the garment of peace provides a solace that comes from Christ alone. In John 14:27, Christ told His disciples that He would give them peace, not the peace of the world, but His peace. That kind of peace is reserved for the one who follows Christ. The peace of God does not allow anger to dwell in its presence. Those things that are not of peace cannot abide in the presence of peace.

When the spirit of anger controls a person, she is often upset with others for little or no reason. The tendency to become irritable and hostile is increased where there is no real focus on Christ. A person who has been angry over periods of time has not allowed anger to resolve (Psalm 37:8), which could lead to other unpleasant situations. The one who is in a state or flux of anger is not at peace and lacks the calmness needed to move past the anger. Christ is the Prince of Peace and where He abides, confusion, hostility, and anger cannot occupy space. The negative spirit of anger develops in places through which the light of Christ is not allowed to shine. Christ is the light. He drives out all darkness.

Unresolved anger can cause a person to become depressed and despondent. We are told in the Bible to not let the sun go down on our anger (Ephesians 4:26). By not allowing ourselves to hold anger throughout the night, we free ourselves of the unnecessary burden of holding on to something that has no positive benefit for us. We have enough happening over the course of 24 hours that we do not need to carry or hold over feelings that are negative and counterproductive.

Unresolved conflict can also cause a person to have extended anger. When a person does not deal with conflict in her life, she will often become angry for what appears to be no reason. Constantly holding on to anger that resulted from a situation and not confronting the issues, persons, or conditions that gave rise to the conflict will often leave the person on high anger alert, which does not allow for resolution. Many times, such continued situations of unresolved conflict can lead to physical problems.

During our lives, we will experience unpleasant situations which may cause us to become angry. With that anger, we may also recall unpleasant memories associated with the event. Unless dealt with effectively, unpleasant memories will replay over and over in a person's mind so many times that she may become agitated at the mention or inference of a person or event. Our bodies are not built to retain anger. Scripture tells us to not hold on to anger, which is why we are told to not carry anger over to another day.

As Christian women, when we deal with situations of our own anger, we would do well to remember that we have support from the Scriptures, which will have calming effects on us, allowing those feelings of hostility to be diminished. When experiencing situations that cause us to become angry, we should go in our minds to a place of "happy thoughts" and think on good things (Philippians 4:8). Using the techniques of renewed thinking, we should focus our thoughts on things that bring us joy and not dwell on the circumstances that cause us frustration. When we allow negative thoughts to linger, they can become so intense that they cause us to act out in ways not becoming a Christian. Prayer allows us to bring our thoughts captive and lay them at the "feet of Jesus" who can control our negative thought patterns because He has already captured the thing that wants to capture us (Ephesians 4:8).

If the negative thoughts are not dealt with effectively, the person could be brought into anger captivity through the continued process of negative thinking. Such thinking allows strongholds to develop and sends the person into a spiraling down pattern. Thank God, we have an advocate who has captured the thing that tries to capture us. Our elder brother, Jesus Christ, has already paid the price for us to be set free from captivity through His victory over death by His resurrection (1 Corinthians 15:51-58).

Prayer is always in order, no matter what the circumstances may present. For Christians, a talk with God is the best solution for any problem. Talking with God allows us to empty ourselves before Him—all of the anger, hurt, hostility, and pain—so that He can fill us with His peace. God does not require anything of us but a contrite spirit and an attitude of submission (James 4:6). God's grace is sufficient for any problem, concern, or spirit that might want to cause us discomfort. Humbly bowing before God, yielding our will to His, and asking for His mercy is what the person who suffers from an anger problem must practice (James 4:2).

Praying Past the Anger

Dear Lord,

I come before You at this time beseeching Your guidance, healing, and direction as I face this spirit of anger that wants to dominate my actions as I respond to those who have hurt me. Please take away the pain that now surrounds me as a result of what has happened, and replace it with the joy of Your love. I know, dear Lord, that I am not able to bear this burden alone—so I am bringing it to You for Your resolve and solace. Search me, Lord, and remove from me any thoughts or feelings that might hinder this prayer. In faith and in the mighty name of Jesus, I do pray this prayer and ask Your healing of my thoughts.

Dear Lord,

Once more I come to ask Your relief in the situation that I now find myself. Lord, I know there is a lesson here for me to learn; please help me to learn it so that I do not have to experience again the pain that goes with anger. Help me to read Your Word more diligently and rely on Your peace that You offer me. Guide me, Lord, in my decisions, and help me know to do things that will cause the spirit of anger to flee from me and allow Your peace to dominate my life. If you find anything in me now, dear Lord, that should not be, please remove it so that this prayer is not hindered. Praying, hoping, and believing in the name of my Lord and Savior, Jesus Christ.

Dear Lord,

I come to You, thanking You for all that You have done for me in the past, with the knowledge that You, again, will lead me through this valley experience. Because I yielded to my own emotions, giving them permission to run ahead of the wisdom that You provide for me, I have allowed myself to be embroiled in anger. Please relieve me of this emotion as I confess to You my sin of unforgiveness that has led to this state of anger. Help me, Lord, please, to let go of those things that have hurt me, and let me seek Your direction as I move through the situations impacting my life. Please give me the peace that You have offered through Your Word—that peace that passes all understanding. Please Lord, remove any negative thoughts or attitudes from me so that this prayer is not hindered. This prayer I bring before you in the name of Your precious Son, Jesus who gave His life to save a wretch like me. In the mighty, matchless, wonderful name of Jesus—Amen!

Tips for Improving My Prayer Life

1. **Pray for wisdom.** As Christians, we have an unending source of wisdom available to us through the One who knows and controls all things (James 1:5). God knows that we are limited in our abilities, after all He made us and He knows all about us. All we have to do is to ask Him for wisdom, and He will not make us feel bad because we ask.

2. **Pray the promises of God.** God is faithful and fulfills His Word. His promises are in His Word, and He never goes back on His Word. Anything that the Lord has promised will come to be (Isaiah 55:11).

3. **Read and meditate on the word of God.** We are told in Scripture that those who meditate on the Word of God will be blessed (Psalm 1:1-6). We are further told that when our minds are focused on God, He will keep us in perfect peace (Isaiah 26:3).

4. **Pray at least three times a day.** Prayer is always appropriate, and we should utilize its benefits continuously. David said that God's Word would continually be in his mouth (Psalm 34:1). Daniel prayed three times a day, even though he was in captivity and praying to God had been forbidden by the King of Medea (Daniel 6:10). We are to pray without ceasing and pray about all things, knowing that we should be thankful in all situations (1 Thessalonians 5:16-18).

5. **Pray focused prayers.** When we pray, we need to identify the area of need and ask the Lord for His blessings upon us. The prayers should be earnest and sincere, laying out before God our situation and requesting His guidance, deliverance, and intervention in the situation (Psalm 35).

6. **Have a prayer partner.** Having a person to agree and pray with you regarding a situation adds strength to the prayer. Praying by large groups of people is demonstrated in the Bible, and the results were favorable for those who prayed (2 Chronicles 20; Esther 4:15-17). In the book of James, we find that Christians are to pray for one another because the prayers of the righteous "availeth much" (James 5:16).

7. **Begin the Seven-Day, Seven-Week Prayer Vigil.** Praying to God through Jesus Christ is a privilege and has positive impact on situations. Seven is considered to be

the number of completion demonstrated many times in the Bible (2 Kings 5:14); a multiple of the days that Daniel prayed and fasted (Daniel 10); and Jesus used as an example of how many times one should be forgiven (Matthew 18:22).

Discussion Questions:

1. When a person is angry, who is in control?
2. Do you know what triggers your anger?
3. Did you know how anger could negatively impact your physical body?
4. What impact does the demonstration of anger by a Christian have on the church?
5. How can you help your sister deal with her anger?
6. Name a Bible character whose anger got the best of him.
7. List seven Scriptures identified in this chapter that deal with anger.

REPLACING ANXIETY WITH MEDITATION

Time that is spent worrying would be better spent meditating on the Word. Our minds are renewed through the Word, and solutions to problems can be found in the Word of God.

CHAPTER FIVE
REPLACING ANXIETY WITH MEDITATION

As we try to live Christian lives, we will constantly be faced with the attacks of satan. He increases his attacks when he sees that we are trying to become stronger in our faith. Satan uses every tactic he can find to control us. He confuses situations and brings doubt, which can cause a person to become anxious or overwhelmed with circumstances. Satan rejoices to see us in the state of anxiousness because this keeps us from focusing on things that are pleasing to God. The only state bigger than the state of anxiety is the state of confusion, which is also of the devil.

The person who is anxious or worried about life's problems becomes susceptible to physical attacks that are orchestrated by the devil. Worry, doubt, and confusion cause our bodies to be in a state of unease. If we follow what Scripture tells us, we will not worry about any situation but will trust God for a resolve (Philippians 4:6-7). We will have fewer headaches, stomachaches, and other aches. When faced with trying situations, we need to turn to God who can relieve us of all our problems. We should "not worry about anything but pray about everything." When we pray sincerely, asking God to direct us and thanking him on the front end for the deliverance we know He can provide, we demonstrate to God our faith in situations for which we can see no solutions (Proverbs 3:5-6).

46

Anxiety may take the form of worry causing uneasiness about minor situations. Worry is a spirit of the devil because if we worry, we aren't meditating on the Word. Spiritual meditation and worry are not compatible because the one who meditates on the Word does not have time to worry. Some people say they do not have time to meditate because they have too much to worry about. My advice to them is to turn your worry time into meditation time. The benefits will be most amazing.

Meditation on the Scriptures generates an atmosphere of calm and peace within our minds. Peace is the best prescription for anxiety. Applied peace will cause the anxious muscles to relax, the rapidly beating heart to calm, and the perspiring foreheads to cool down. Throughout the book of Psalms, we find encouraging, uplifting passages that can provide comfort and relief to the troubled soul (Psalm 1; Psalm 91; Psalm 100; Psalm 121).

Picturing images of pleasant experiences and joyful events can often cause a person to become at ease and less anxious. Having good thoughts and remembering happy times and relationships are ways of countering feelings of anxiousness or worry. Panic attacks set in when there is apprehension, fear, or distress associated with a particular activity. Praying to God and asking Him to help guide us through those difficult times is a practice that should be a part of our spiritual defense as Christian women (John 15:7).

Anxious thoughts can have a physical impact on our bodies. If left unattended, we can become ill. Our thoughts control our body functions. If someone tells us that a hungry lion is just the other side of the door, the heart will begin fast palpitations; sweat glands will begin secretion; the body temperature will increase; and fear and anxiety would set in—all because of the thought of a hungry lion on the other side of the door. Our levels of anxiety would build; body organs would respond to the fear of a lion; and our brains would prepare us for "fight or flight." The devil knows what it takes to get us to respond in a way that undermines how we know we should respond. Sometimes, the devil causes someone to lie to us just to see our reaction to that toxic thought.

When someone is in a constant state of anxiousness, over time, she will be negatively impacted by the continuous influx of adrenalin secretions that are not expended through body activity. Replacing anxious thoughts with peaceful thoughts allows the body to go to "relax mode" as opposed to "high-alert mode." We are told continuously in the Bible to guard our minds and not to worry or be anxious about anything (Isaiah 26:3; Proverbs 4:23; Luke 12:26-28; Philippians 4:6).

Knowing and applying Scripture will help us control those anxious thoughts and curtail some of our physical problems. Anxious-free thoughts are facilitated through a reliance on the Word and a focus on God (Isaiah 26:3).

Worry, which is a form of anxiety, is also a trick of the devil. He causes us to worry about situations over which we often have little or no control. Satan delights in our worrying because when we're worrying, we do not have time to pray or meditate about what God would have us to do. If the solution does fall within our realm of control, then we should act decisively to solve the situation. However, if the solution is clearly not within our area of control, we should meditate on possible solutions, pray about it, ask God to resolve it—believing that He will resolve it, then move on to the next situation that needs addressing. If satan can get us stuck in the stupor of worry, he feels as if he is winning the battle. However, before the devil becomes too comfortable in the mess he has created for you, begin to send up your requests with prayers of thanksgiving to God for resolving the situation, and satan will have to find other ground to plant his seeds of worry and doubt (James 4:7). Remember, you are "too blessed to tolerate satan's mess."

In the difficult situations in which we live today, we find that people will disappoint us by failing to deliver on commitments they have made. As a result, we may worry about whether to continue in an effort when it looks like all signs point to abandoning the idea. That is the time when the Christian should dig in with prayer and determination because the battle is almost won. Satan knows that, so he "turns up the heat" on problems, causing fear, doubt, and anxiety. But the Christian woman should pull on her knowledge of God and how He has brought many a follower through adverse situations. This is not the time for her to become anxious but the time to give thanks to God for trusting her to deal with this particular situation, remembering with Christ's help, she can do all things (Philippians 4:13).

There are times when sisters can help sisters through situations by just lending a listening ear. A word of encouragement or concern from a fellow sister is often needed by one who is suffering from worry or doubt (Proverbs 25:11). Single mothers may become anxious regarding their children and the problems they may be facing. Not knowing how to deal with a teenager or not having the time to go to the school and deal with problems that may occur can cause the young mother to become anxious and worried. Older sisters can help younger sisters in dealing with difficult situations through showing acts of kindness by sharing life experiences and building relationships (Titus 2:3-4).

Worry is one of the ploys that satan uses to get us to lose faith. All kinds of "what if" thoughts invade our minds and cause us to question various aspects of our faith. When satan can get us to second guess our positive efforts, he is happy, because he is planting the seed of doubt, which will hinder the progress in achieving a goal. This is when the Christian needs to rest in the Lord and not doubt what is good (James 1:6).

Rather than worry or become anxious about a situation, we need to remember that we should "not worry about anything but pray about everything" (Philippians 4:6). Worry will not change anything except our ability to be at peace. The Bible tells us to cast our cares on the Lord and know that God is in control (Psalm 55:22).

Meditation on God's Word and reflecting on the many times He delivered those who were in peril should help us to know that God will be there for us today. He will deliver us from trouble and do for us what He did for those of old. This should renew our spirits and remove our doubts (Hebrews 13:8). Trusting and believing God's Word keeps us from fear and doubt. Reading the Scriptures helps us to meditate and know that Christ wants us to have His peace and wants us to walk in faith, not doubt (2 Corinthians 5:7). Doubt is the cloud that comes to hang over the Christian to steal her joy by causing her to question things that she has learned regarding the role Christ plays in her life. When she feels that cloud coming over her she should make haste to the Bible and read the words of the Master. By reading and meditating on the Word of God, the Christian resists the devil by filling her mind with God's Word rather than satan's doubts. The devil cannot dwell in a mind filled with the Word of God (James 4:7).

Discussion Questions:

1. What are some of the causes of worry?
2. How does satan work to cause Christians to worry?
3. What are some indicators that a person may be anxious about a situation?
4. How can we encourage our Christian women to know the importance of meditation?
5. How can the church help those who are struggling?
6. How can older senior sisters become more involved in helping younger sisters?
7. Discuss seven Scriptures in this chapter that can provide comfort to the one who is suffering from anxiety.

CONQUERING DEPRESSION BY A FOCUS ON TRUTH

One of the devil's hardest tricks to overcome is that of depression, which often is a result of lies, violence, and/or disappointment. The truth of God is the best antidote for the lie of satan and feelings of worthlessness that want to invade the mind.

CHAPTER 6
CONQUERING DEPRESSION BY A FOCUS ON TRUTH

There has been a surge of violence in our cities and towns. These violent acts cause unrest, heightened stress, fear, and depression among our citizens. The devil is busy using the spirits of deception, hostility, envy, and hate to lure minds into believing there is no hope for peace and tranquility. Children go to school after seeing horrific situations occurring on television, in their neighborhoods, and even in their homes. Individuals commit violent acts because of lies they may have been told, and innocent people become victims. School children witness the commission of violent crimes on their school grounds. All of those have their origin in the acts and wiles of the devil. The devil is happiest when he knows that people are so focused on the violent, negative acts that are happening, they forget to remember they can intervene through petitioning God regarding those situations (Psalm 34:17).

If satan can get people to believe that other people are against them and are deliberately doing mean things to them, or if he convinces youths that to be accepted they must be a part of a gang, then he is achieving his goal "by any means necessary," and he is quite happy. The devil is plotting for the lives of our children and to destroy our families. He is carrying out his mission "to kill, steal and destroy" (John 10:10). This is spiritual warfare that the devil has unleased on God's people to cause them not to seek God, but to seek vengeance.

Living in conditions such as described above will often cause a person to become depressed. Not knowing where danger may be, who could be out to do them harm, whether violence will erupt in the neighborhood, or how they will sustain lifestyles in the face of economic depression all give rise to negative thought patterns. When negative thoughts constantly bombard our minds, we become depressed, despondent, and uneasy. Proverbs 4:23 tells us to guard our minds since that is where the sources of life are found. Once we begin the negative thought process, we begin to descend into a place of depression. When depression is allowed to continue without spiritual intervention, one may begin to question her existence. As Christians, we must not let those toxic thoughts take hold of our spiritual being because we are "more than conquerors" and are blessed to be in right relationship with God (Romans 8:37).

Most acts of violence can be traced to anger and deception—both tools of the devil. The young person who is deceived into thinking that to have money, he must take it from someone else has been grossly deceived. Satan will contrive a lie, dress it up so well, that he can even try to fool saints of God (Matthew 24:4). For the husband or the wife, the suspicion of infidelity causes each to focus on the negatives and can cause unrest or violence in the home. In neighborhoods, rivalries can occur when some friends are closer than others and begin to tell ugly things about one another. In government, officials may not always be forthright regarding various issues. Their constituents may become upset as a result. All those situations can cause persons to become despondent or reactionary, violent or depressed. A closer look will reveal the devil and his lies are at the base of the problem (John 8:44).

Depression can set in when we concentrate on all the problems that we may have or how others have betrayed us. Continuously thinking about all of the things that are bad in our lives causes negative thoughts to build on negative thoughts. Soon, you have a mountain of negativity that looms over the person.

Deception, and lies, which play a large role in depression, (two of the chief ploys of satan), must be dealt with so that situations my improve. In the home, in the neighborhood, and in the political arena, **truth must be told.** Why? When looking at the way Christians are to be prepared to stand against the spiritual attacks of the devil, truth is listed as the first weapon of warfare (Ephesians 6:14). The belt of truth is listed first in the series of armor that the Christian must have in this spiritual war. "Truth is the best defense against a lie," and it stands when all else falls. Jesus told us "ye shall know the truth and the truth will make you free" (John 8:32). Truth frees the person of fear, which is a spirit of bondage. Truth allows the person to move freely in interacting with others and opens the door to understanding.

When lies have been told and individuals have become depressed or despondent under the weight of those lies, truth is refreshing to the that person. Truth will relieve those feelings of worthlessness and sadness. In the state of depression, the person can become victim to toxic negative thinking. Truth unmasks a lie and shows it for what it is worth—nothing.

The Christian can provide encouragement to the one who is in depression by sharing the love and concern that God has for that person. Knowing that "God loves us even when we don't love ourselves" helps the person to know that God's love is unconditional. Helping the person to know that God can strengthen her, even in the worst times, is a comforting reality (Isaiah 41:10) and that having "right thinking" is something that can belong to all.

Depression is a stronghold of the devil and feeds on negative thinking. Our thoughts form the basis of our actions. The thought that is negative and goes unchecked can become an attitude, which then becomes a behavior that can result in a stronghold. God is able to break every yoke and stronghold that wants to entangle us. When a thought comes to mind that is a violation of God's Word, we need to "bring it into the obedience of Christ" (2 Corinthians 10:5). We should replace negative thoughts with positive thoughts and not allow our minds to dwell on toxic thoughts. Negative thinking is a strong part of depression.

Exposing ourselves to the truth of God's Word is something that should be done daily. Meditating on the Scriptures fortifies the mind with the essentials of life. By knowing God's Word, we can respond to satan and his temptations in the manner that Jesus responded, "It is written...." (Matthew 4:4).

God's Word is truth and life (John 6:63). Jesus declared that He is the truth and the life (John 14:6), and we know that we have freedom in Jesus because He is truth. For the one who is depressed, despondent, and forlorn, I would recommend to you Jesus, because He cares for His own (1 Peter 5:7).

Discussion Questions:

1. What are some of the causes of depression?

2. Why is it not healthy to remain in depression?

3. What kind of problems can develop when people become depressed over long periods of time?

4. What are some of the signs of depression?

5. Discuss how truth exposes deception and what results when deception meets truth.

6. How can sisters assist others in overcoming depression?

7. List seven Scriptures that would be helpful to remember when dealing with depression.

"THE CONCLUSION OF THE WHOLE MATTER"

The devil is waging war against Christians. He wants us to lose our focus on God and do the things that are contrary to God's will. Christians must remain vigilant, focused, and clothed with the full armor of God!

CHAPTER SEVEN

"LET US HEAR THE COCLUSION OF THE WHOLE MATTER" ECCLESIASTIES 12:13

Satan knows that his time is running out, therefore, he has launched a full-scale assault on the world to try to take as many people to hell with him as he can. We have been told in Scripture that he is like a "roaring lion, seeking whom he may devour" (1 Peter 5:8), and we do not want to be the devil's next meal. He especially wants to lure Christians to him because he knows that it hurts God to see His children stray. The devil is a liar and deceiver, and he is using every ploy he can to win people to him.

When brothers and sisters cannot get along in the home and even the church, know that satan is on the loose, trying to steal minds so that he can win souls for his kingdom of darkness. Resisting the devil is key to defeating him in his efforts to recruit followers (James 4:7). If we want to put satan on the run, we need to use the Bible. The Scriptures cause satan to be most uncomfortable, so when you read the word of God, quote Scriptures, and live by God's commandments, you put satan on notice, and he isn't comfortable in that environment. Be not angry with your brother nor your sister when he or she acts in a negative manner. Know that satan is trying to have his way with that person and causes strife and confusion at every opportunity (1 Corinthians 14:33). As Christians, we can overcome satan by the words we use and the fact that we have the blood of Christ, which covers us and shields us (Revelation 12:11).

Solomon, who was the wisest man who ever lived, concluded long ago that the "whole duty of man is to serve God and keep His commandments" (Ecclesiastes 12:13). That conclusion was true then and is true even now.

Almost from the beginning of time, man has not wanted to follow God's instructions (Genesis 2:16-17). Man, under the influence of satan, has sought ways to avoid doing what the Lord would have him to do. These acts of going against God's will, or rebellion, have continued even into this age, and we see no sign of things improving. Sin forms the basis of mankind's rebellion against the teachings of God. Satan uses our lusts (lust of the eye, lust of the flesh, and the pride of life—1 John 2:16) to lead us into sin. When we are led away, we become spiritually weak and headed for destruction.

God is a forgiving God and always wants His people to return to Him. God is love and wants all to be saved eternally to live with Him. If we would put our faith in God, rely on His promises, and do His will, we would be so much better and happier (2 Corinthians 7:14). Without the act of repentance, "sin for a season jeopardizes life for an eternity."

God does not want any of us to perish but wants us all to repent and be saved (2 Peter 3:9). Many times, God uses others to cause individuals to return to Him. As we interact with people on a daily basis, we often find that they are living sinful lives and are miserable in the process. This is because they know what they are doing is not right and a voice of conscience pulls at them to return to God (the Spirit is working), but they refuse to return. It may be that we must take the initiative to show interest in that person's well-being. Although they may not be willing to "hear" a sermon, they are usually receptive to "seeing" a sermon. Thus, the lives we live before others can have bearing on whether they choose to become obedient to the Word of God.

It is not unusual for women to sometimes become envious of other women who they think are living better than they. In doing this, some become hostile to others with no basis for the hostility other than their own imaginations. Souls needing salvation could be turned away simply by the attitudes and behaviors demonstrated by those who profess to be Christians. We must be mindful that our dispositions can impact the response that is given to the call of salvation. Those who look at women who are professing Christianity should see Christ reflecting in our lives.

Our positive, non-retaliatory actions may be just the catalyst needed to help that person turn toward God. Isaiah, long ago, answered the call of helping the people of God see their wicked ways (Isaiah 6:8). People see situations happening today and say, "Somebody ought to do something." Well, you just may be that somebody. You may have to be the one to say, "Here am I; send me." And just like Esther, you may have been sent for "such a time as this" (Esther 4:14). Persons who can demonstrate genuine interest in the needs of someone else may be able to bring that individual to Christ.

Fear, anger, anxiety, and depression are all major ploys of satan. Fear is an imposter and wants to take the place of faith. Faith will sustain you when conquering obstacles and overcoming mountains of problems. Your faithfulness during a trying situation demonstrates to God that you believe and trust Him for the resolve of all of life's problems. God has a history of being faithful concerning His promises to man (Joshua 1:9; II Kings 20:17; 1 Corinthians 1:9). God has endured the test of time, and God, who is the Creator of time, will determine when time will be no more. Fear tries to convince the Christian that God will not deliver her from the problems she may face. However, faith stands boldly and declares that God has prevailed over all situations time and time again, and there is no force powerful enough to defy the will of God (Isaiah 14:24).

Christ has told us that He will make us "fishers of men" (Matthew 4:19). There are those who are tossing on the sea of life and are perishing because of lack of faith, a rebellious spirit, and/or refusing to adhere to the teachings of God. Many are crying for salvation, longing to be fed, and we must respond, "Here am I, send me" (Isaiah 6:8).

By responding to the needs of others, we demonstrate love for our neighbor, and in doing so, we are following God the Son's commandments (Mark 12:30-31). Jesus wants us to obey His commandments and love others, living in a manner so that they will know we are His (John 13:35).

Discussion Questions:

1. Do you demonstrate to others that you are concerned about their spiritual well-being?

2. Would someone on your job see you as a "practicing Christian"?

3. How many times have you invited someone to attend worship with you?

4. Have you ever had a Bible study with someone who was wanting to know more about Christ?

5. Have you ever participated in a Bible Table Talk discussion?

6. What is man's main responsibility?

7. List and discuss seven Scriptures in this chapter that will be helpful along this Christian journey.

APPENDIX
A PERSONAL PRAYER OF THANKSGIVING FOR HEALING

Below is a prayer I have written, which is based on Scriptures and specifically focused on healing. It can be prayed by many for a specific person and allows the pray-er to center on the awesomeness of God's ability to heal any and all areas of our being. This prayer was written based on faith and the knowledge that God is the God of healing. The prayer affirms for the pray-er that God is faithful and wants His children to be well. Sickness is not of God but healing is one of God's blessings. Jesus is the Great Physician and the Christian can rest on the affirmation that "by His stripes we are healed" (Isaiah 53:5).

Dear Lord,

As I meditate on these Scriptures today and pray to you about my condition, I ask that You heal me and allow my days of health to be restored. It is with faith in You, God, that I prayer this prayer of faith for healing, and with faith I meditate on these Scriptures; believing what the Scriptures say:

It is written in Matthew 21:21, "Verily, I say unto you, if ye have faith, and doubt not, ye shall not only do this which is done to the fig tree, but also, if ye shall say unto this mountain, Be thou removed and be thou cast into the sea, it will be done." And so, believing the words of our Lord and not doubting, I say to this mountain of sickness that is coming against me: Be removed and be cast into the sea.

God, I know You are faithful to Your promises. Deuteronomy 7:15 says, "And the Lord will take way from thee all thy sickness...." So, dear Lord, I ask You to take away this sickness from me and restore me to good health.

Being a child of God has many benefits and healing is one of those benefits. Psalm 103:1-5 says, " Bless the Lord, O my soul; and all that is within me bless His Holy Name. Bless the Lord, O my soul and forget not all His benefits; Who forgiveth all thine iniquities and who healeth all thy diseases; who redeemeth thy life from destruction, who crowneth thee with loving kindness and tender mercies. Who satisfieth thy mouth with good things, so that thy youth is renewed like the eagle's." God, I thank You for the benefit of healing.

As I am praying this prayer and meditating, I remember Psalm 118:17 says, "I shall not die but live and declare the works of the Lord." So, Lord, I ask You to take away this illness that wants to manifest in my body; it has no right to be here, and so in the name of Jesus I command it to leave.

As was told by the writer of Proverbs, the words of the Father are health and healing: Proverbs 4:20-23 says, "My son attend to my words; incline thine ear unto my sayings. Let them not depart from thine eyes; keep them in the midst of thine heart; For they are life unto those that find them and health to all their flesh."

God, I trust You to fulfill the promise of help. Isaiah 41:10 says "Fear thou not; for I am with thee; be not dismayed for I am thy God; I will strengthen thee; yea; I will help thee; yea I will uphold thee with my right hand of my righteousness." And so, dear Lord I believe that promise— that You will strengthen me and uphold me.

God, Your promises are true, and Your healing is sure: I know that You said in Jeremiah 30:17 "...I will restore health unto thee, and I will heal thee of thy wounds...." I know that promise applies to me, and I accept it.

I want to speak words of life, and when I cannot speak them aloud, I will speak them in my mind—the words of the Lord. Joel 3:10 tells us ...let the weak say I am strong." Dear Lord, I am strong through thee because it is written that "I can do all things through Christ Jesus who strengthens me" (Philippians 4:13).

I know that Jesus does not want me to be sick. He healed everyone who asked and everyone who had an intercessor asking: I am asking, Dear Lord, and I know that I have intercessors asking and believing for my healing. So, we ask according to Matthew 7:7, "Ask and it shall be given unto you." We ask, and I receive the healing that is occurring right now in my body.

The Word of God is perfect and provides inspiration. Second Timothy 3:16 says, "All Scripture is given by the inspiration of God and is profitable for doctrine, for reproof, for correction for instruction in righteousness." I apply the Scriptures, the Word, to my sickness and know that healing is mine.

I know that when we pray, we must believe and not doubt. Hebrews 10:23 says "Let us hold fast the profession of our faith without wavering for He is faithful that promised."

When Christians pray, we know Lord, that You hear us. First John 5:15 says, "And if we know that he hears us, whatsoever we ask, we know that we have the petitions that we desired of him." And now dear Lord, I thank You for the healing that is mine and Your blessing of health.

I know dear Lord, that when I cry unto You, You will help me. It is written in Psalm 30:2, "O Lord my God, I cried unto thee, and thou hast healed me." God, I know that You will save Your own. Psalm 107:19 tells me, "Then they cry unto the Lord in their trouble, and he saveth them out of their distresses."

I know God, that when you make a promise, it happens and Your promises to us are yes. Second Corinthians 1:20 tells me, "For all the promises of God in Him are yea, and in him Amen, unto the glory of God by us."

Lord, I will praise You at all times and give thanks to You for Your mercies. Psalm 69:30 says, "I will praise the name of God with a song, and will magnify him with thanksgiving" and Psalm 100:4-5 says, " ...be thankful unto him and bless his name. For the Lord is good, his mercy is everlasting and his truth endureth to all generations."

Jesus took away our sins and healed our diseases. I rejoice in the knowledge of Isaiah 53:5, which says, "...with His stripes we are healed'. Lord, I know You hear and answer my prayers. I believe Isaiah 65:24, which says, "And it shall come to pass, that before they call I will answer, and while they yet speak—I will hear." Lord, I thank You for hearing my prayers.

As a Christian, I have the comfort of knowing that You, God, are the only One who offers peace, even in the midst of a storm. Philippians 4:6-7 instructs me: "Be careful for nothing, but in everything through prayer and supplication with thanksgiving, let your requests be made known unto God. And the peace of God, which passeth all understanding shall keep your hearts and minds through Christ Jesus." Lord, right now, I am in a storm—a storm of sickness—and I am trusting that You will see me safely through this storm, restore my health, and give me that peace that we read about in the Bible: the peace that passes all understanding.

John 15:7 tells me, "If ye abide in me, and my words abide in you, ye shall ask what you will and it shall be done unto you." Lord, I am abiding in You, and Your Word abides in me, so with that confession I ask You for the healing of my body. LORD, I THANK YOU FOR MY HEALING!

And so, Dear God, it is with prayer, supplication, and thanksgiving that I make my request known to you. I know that I will conquer this sickness and that it will not have dominion over me because through Christ Jesus, I am more than a conqueror. It is in the mighty name of Jesus that I pray Your promises; believe Your Word; and receive Your healing—In the mighty, matchless, wonderful name of JESUS—Amen and Amen.